HIROSHIMA AND NAGASAKI

Lynn Peppas

Crabtree Publishing
crabtreebooks.com

Crabtree Publishing

crabtreebooks.com 800-387-7650

In Canada: We acknowledge the financial support of the Government of Canada through the Canada Book Fund for our publishing activities.

Author: Lynn Peppas
Publishing plan research and development: Reagan Miller
Editors: Sonya Newland, Kathy Middleton
Proofreader: Crystal Sikkens
Photo Researchers: Sonya Newland
Original design: Tim Mayer (Mayer Media) Book design: Kim Williams (320 Media)
Cover design: Ken Wright
Production manager: Candice Campbell
Prepress technician: Katherine Kantor

Produced for Crabtree Publishing Company by White-Thomson Publishing

Hardcover 978-0-7787-1171-1
Paperback 978-0-7787-1179-7
Ebook (pdf) 978-1-4271-8924-0

Printed in the U.S.A./062025/CP20250603

Published in Canada
Crabtree Publishing
616 Welland Avenue
St. Catharines, Ontario
L2M 5V6

Published in the United States
Crabtree Publishing
347 Fifth Avenue
Suite 1402-145
New York, NY 10016

Photographs: Alamy: Everett Collection Historical: pp. 1, 18–19. Corbis: Bettmann: pp. 16–17, 30–31, 34, 43; John Van Hasselt/Sygma: p. 28. Getty Images: pp. 14, 22; Time & Life Pictures: pp. 8–9, 10–11; AFP: pp. 38–39. Library of Congress: pp. 12–13, 32–33. Shutterstock: J.D.S: pp. 14–15; SeanPavonePhoto: pp. 40–41; Mary416: p. 41; Paolo Gianti: p. 42; Dmitry Kalinovsky: pp. 44–45. SuperStock: p. 4; Pietro Scozzari/age footstock: pp. 3, 35, 36–37; Image Asset Management Ltd: pp. 26–27; Karen Kasmauski/Science Faction: p. 37. USAF: pp. 24–25, 29; Jeff Fisher: p. 23. Wikimedia: p. 32; NARA: pp. 6, 20–21; U.S. Army Corps of Engineers: p. 19; © David Pentland and Cranston Fine Arts: front cover

Library and Archives Canada Cataloguing in Publication
Peppas, Lynn, author
Hiroshima and Nagasaki / Lynn Peppas.
(Crabtree chrome)
Includes index.
Issued in print and electronic formats.
ISBN 978-0-7787-1171-1 (bound).--
ISBN 978-0-7787-1179-7 (pbk.)
ISBN 978-1-4271-8932-5 (pdf).--
ISBN 978-1-4271-8924-0 (html)
1. Hiroshima-shi (Japan)--History--Bombardment, 1945--Juvenile literature. 2. Nagasaki-shi (Japan)--History--Bombardment, 1945--Juvenile literature. 3. World War, 1939-1945--Japan--Hiroshima-shi--Juvenile literature. 4. World War, 1939-1945--Japan--Nagasaki-shi--Juvenile literature. 5. Atomic bomb--Juvenile literature. I. Title. II. Series: Crabtree chrome
D767.25.H6P46 2013 j940.54'2521954 C2013-906222-X
C2013-906223-8

Library of Congress Cataloging-in-Publication Data
CIP available at Library of Congress

壊した
工場から
山の
防空壕へ
らくして
い雨が
タボタと
落ちて
きた
黒い雨

Nuclear Nightmare

▲ *The atomic bomb's mushroom-shaped cloud rose over 9 miles (14.5 kilometers) above the city of Hiroshima.*

A Normal Day?

Monday, August 6, 1945, began like most other days for the 255,000 citizens of Hiroshima, Japan. Around 7 a.m. an **air-raid alarm** sounded. The people of Hiroshima were used to hearing it. Enemy aircraft often flew over the city, but they rarely dropped bombs.

The Bomb Drops

An hour later the all-clear signal sounded, telling the people of Hiroshima they could safely go about their lives. By 8:14 a.m. people were on their way to work. Children were playing outside or getting ready for school. All that changed in a split second when an atomic bomb was dropped on the city. This weapon was more destructive than any other in history.

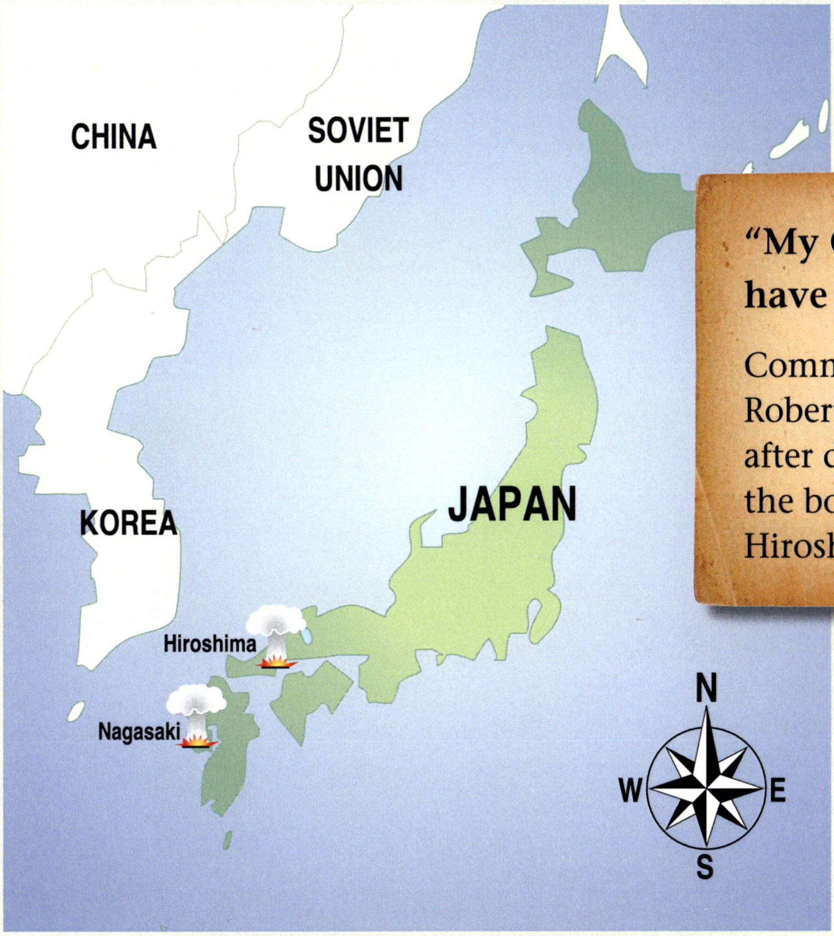

"My God, what have we done?"

Commander Robert Lewis, after dropping the bomb on Hiroshima

▲ *This map shows the Japanese cities of Hiroshima and Nagasaki, where the atomic bombs were dropped in August 1945.*

air-raid alarm: a warning of an air attack during wartime

Atomic Destruction

The atomic bomb—also called a **nuclear** bomb or an A-bomb—was a brand new weapon. It had never been used in a place where large numbers of people lived. It had only been tested in areas where no one lived. When the bomb dropped, it destroyed almost everything within three miles (five kilometers) of ground zero, or the point where it hit.

▼ *The second atomic bomb, dropped on Nagasaki, was called Fat Man. It was powered by plutonium.*

Energy from Atoms

An atomic bomb gets its energy when atoms of heavy metals such as uranium or plutonium are broken or split apart. The splitting of atoms is called fission. In an atomic bomb, fission takes place in one of two ways. Either a bullet of uranium is shot at more uranium (or plutonium) to split the atoms, or the atoms are forced together so violently by an explosive substance that they split apart.

▼ *The first atomic bomb, dropped on Hiroshima, was called Little Boy. It was powered by uranium.*

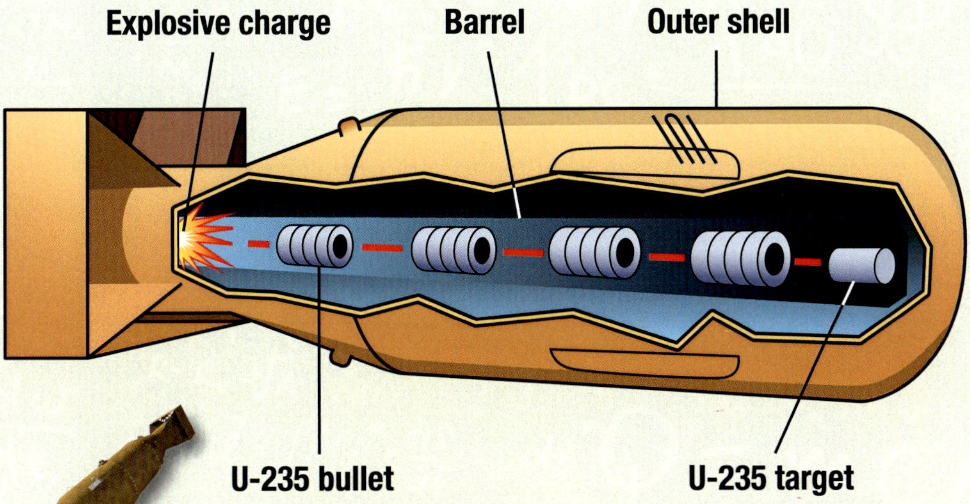

Uranium and plutonium are very heavy metals that occur naturally on Earth. The atoms of some types of these metals give off huge amounts of energy when they are split. This causes a massive explosion.

nuclear: powered by the energy released when atoms collide

The Age of Nuclear Science

Throughout the 1930s, scientists studied nuclear physics—the science of the tiny particles in atoms—in great detail. But it was not until 1938 that a group of German scientists discovered nuclear fission. The best scientists from around the world knew that if they could build a bomb using this science, it would be a hugely powerful weapon. The race was on to create the first atomic bomb.

Potential for Disaster

In August 1939, U.S. president Franklin Roosevelt received a letter from the famous scientist Albert Einstein. In the letter, he described the dreadful **potential** of an atomic bomb. He also explained that German scientists were already working on such a weapon. Roosevelt decided that the United States must build the bomb before Germany did.

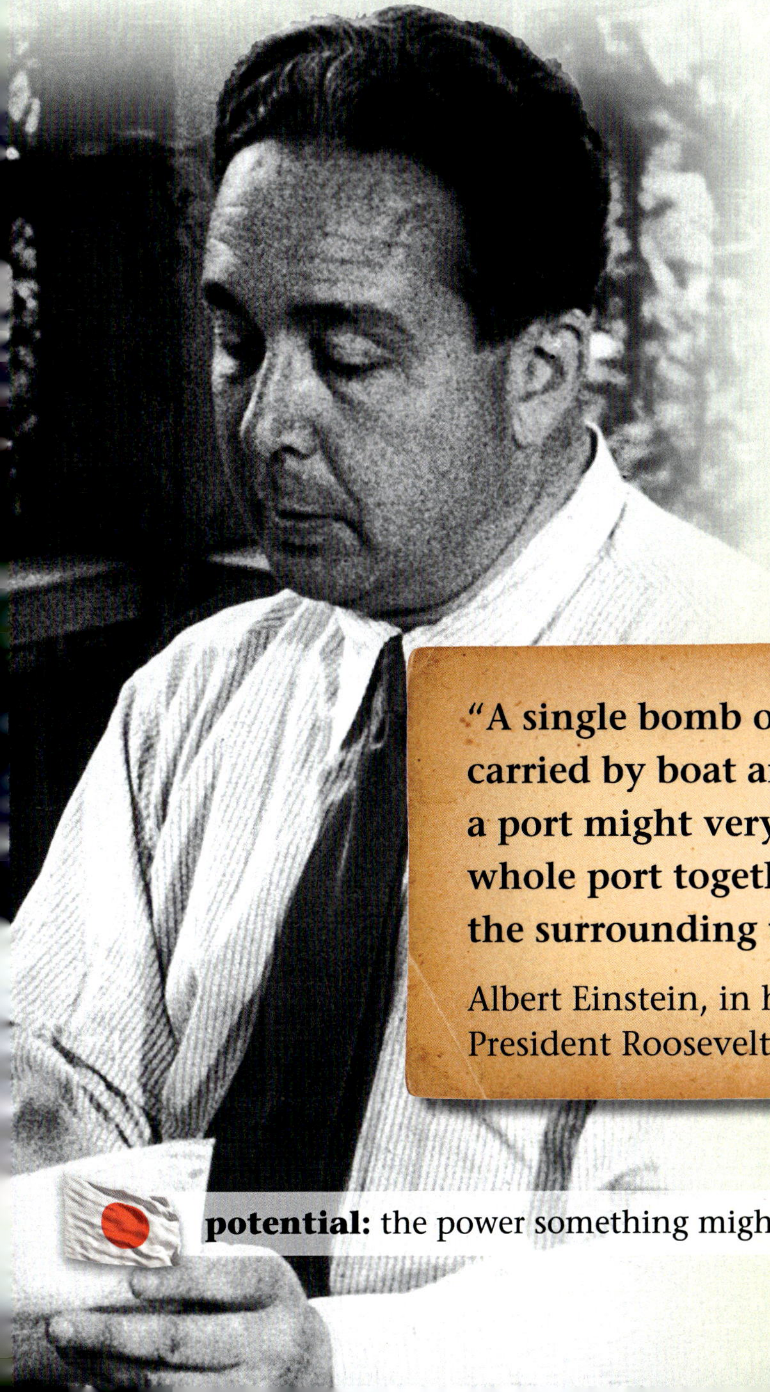

◀ *Hungarian-born scientist Leo Szilard (right) wrote the letter to send to President Roosevelt. He asked Einstein (left) to sign it because Einstein was world famous and greatly respected.*

"A single bomb of this type carried by boat and exploded in a port might very well destroy the whole port together with some of the surrounding territory."

Albert Einstein, in his letter to President Roosevelt

potential: the power something might have in the future

The World at War

War Begins

In the 1930s, there was unrest in Europe. The German leader, Adolf Hitler, wanted to make Germany powerful by taking over other countries. When he invaded Poland in 1939, World War II broke out. Britain, France, Canada, and Russia, known as the Allies, fought against Germany, Japan, and Italy, known as the Axis powers.

Staying out of the War

The United States did not join the war right away. But President Roosevelt kept a careful eye on events in Europe. He was also worried about how much power Japan had. Japan had invaded China, so the United States and other countries placed an oil **embargo** on Japan. Without oil, the Japanese army could not fight for long.

▼ *Adolf Hitler watches German soldiers march through the streets of Poland's capital, Warsaw, after the invasion that triggered World War II.*

World War II is the deadliest war ever fought in terms of numbers killed. More than 50 million people died during the six years that the war lasted. Half of these were soldiers, but the rest were regular citizens.

embargo: a law banning trade with a particular country

Leading to War

For the first two years of the war, the United States remained **neutral**. But the U.S. government helped the Allies by sending them supplies. The Japanese worried that the United States might send troops to stop them from fighting in Asia. To prevent this, Japan planned a secret attack on the United States.

The Battle of Pearl Harbor

On the morning of December 7, 1941, Japan attacked the U.S. naval base at Pearl Harbor in Hawaii. The assault took everyone by surprise. American fighter pilots scrambled to their planes to fight back in the skies. But the damage had already been done. Four battleships were sunk and almost 200 aircraft destroyed. Thousands of soldiers were killed.

▼ *The Japanese bombed U.S. Navy ships, aircraft, and military stationed at Pearl Harbor in the Pacific Ocean.*

> **"Hostilities exist. There is no blinking at the fact that our people, our territory, and our interests are in grave danger ... since Sunday, December 7th, 1941, a state of war has existed between the United States and the Japanese empire."**
>
> President Franklin Roosevelt

neutral: not involved in a conflict

The Race for a Nuclear Weapon

The United States was now drawn into World War II. More than ever, Roosevelt realized the importance of having the most advanced weapons. He and other Allied leaders knew they had to create the atomic bomb first. If German scientists beat them to it, Germany would probably win the war.

▲ *Some of the world's greatest scientists came together to work on the Allied effort to build the atomic bomb. One of the project's leaders was the American J. Robert Oppenheimer.*

The Manhattan Project

In September 1942, scientists from Britain, the United States, and Canada started working together to build the bomb. This was a top-secret project. Hardly anyone knew about it. One of the many places the scientists worked was in New York City, in the **borough** of Manhattan. The operation became known as the Manhattan Project.

◀ *The first ever nuclear reactor was built as part of the Manhattan Project in 1943. It still stands today.*

The United States ended up spending over $2 billion on the Manhattan Project. Most of the money went toward building top-secret plants and producing materials to build the A-bomb.

borough: an area within a city with its own local government

A New President

President Roosevelt died suddenly on April 12, 1945, months before the first atomic bomb was even tested. The vice president, Harry Truman, became president. It was not an easy job to step into suddenly, especially during wartime. The Manhattan Project was so top secret that even Truman did not know about it until he became president.

War Time

World War II was a stormy time in history. Americans at home were dealing with **shortages** in food and supplies because of the war. Finally, on May 8, 1945, the weakened German army surrendered, ending World War II in Europe. But the conflict between the United States and Japan continued.

▼ *These American soldiers are attacking the Japanese island of Iwo Jima. The war in the Pacific region continued after the war in Europe ended.*

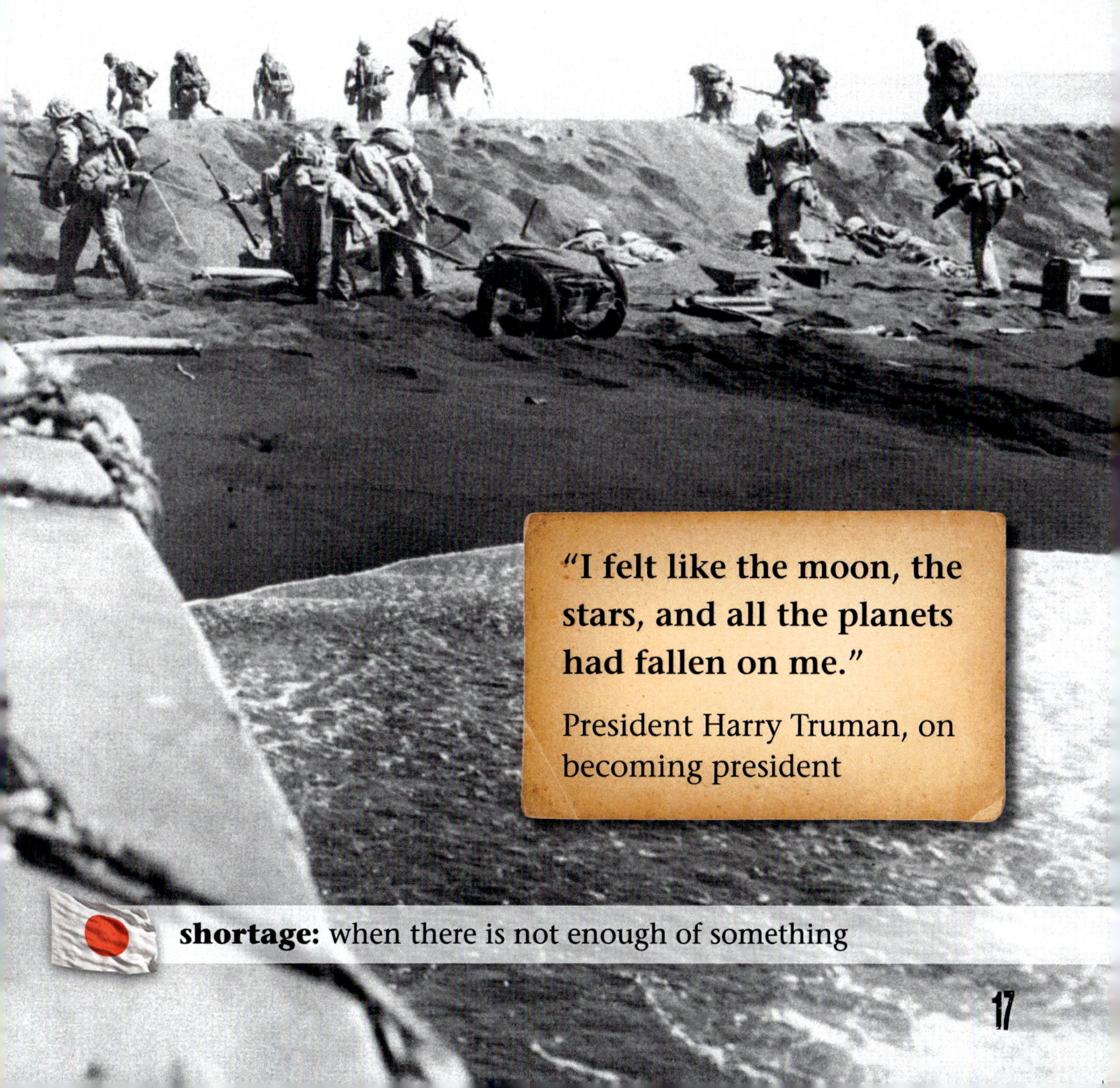

"I felt like the moon, the stars, and all the planets had fallen on me."

President Harry Truman, on becoming president

shortage: when there is not enough of something

The Trinity Test

By mid-July, the Manhattan Project scientists had built a bomb they called "Gadget." They prepared a special site to test it in a remote part of the desert in New Mexico, near Alamogordo. Gadget was lifted to the top of a 100-foot (30-meter) steel tower ready for action. The code name for this atomic bomb test was "Trinity."

▶ *Citizens of New Mexico saw and heard the atomic blast over 100 miles (160 kilometers) away. To explain the huge explosion, army officials released a statement saying that a building filled with ammunition had blown up.*

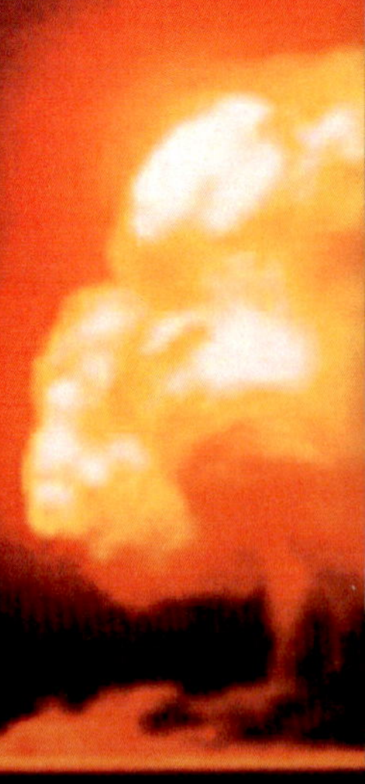

"The heat was like opening up an oven door, even at 10 miles."

A military policeman at base camp 10 miles (16 kilometers) from the test site

▶ *Oppenheimer and fellow scientist Leslie Groves examine what remains of the base of the steel tower after the explosion.*

The First Atomic Explosion

Around 5:30 a.m. on Monday, July 16, 1945, the first-ever atomic bomb explosion occurred. The steel tower **evaporated** instantly, and the explosion created a 1200-foot (366-meter) crater. The heat from the bomb melted the desert sand, turning it into green glass. The explosion was more destructive than any of the scientists could have imagined. The Allies had won the race—they had an atomic weapon.

evaporated: changed from a solid to a gas

The Potsdam Meeting

The same month as the first atomic bomb test took place, Allied leaders met in the city of Potsdam in Germany. The war in Europe was over. Now the victors had to decide how to deal with the defeated nations. They also discussed what to do about Japan, which was still fighting the Allies.

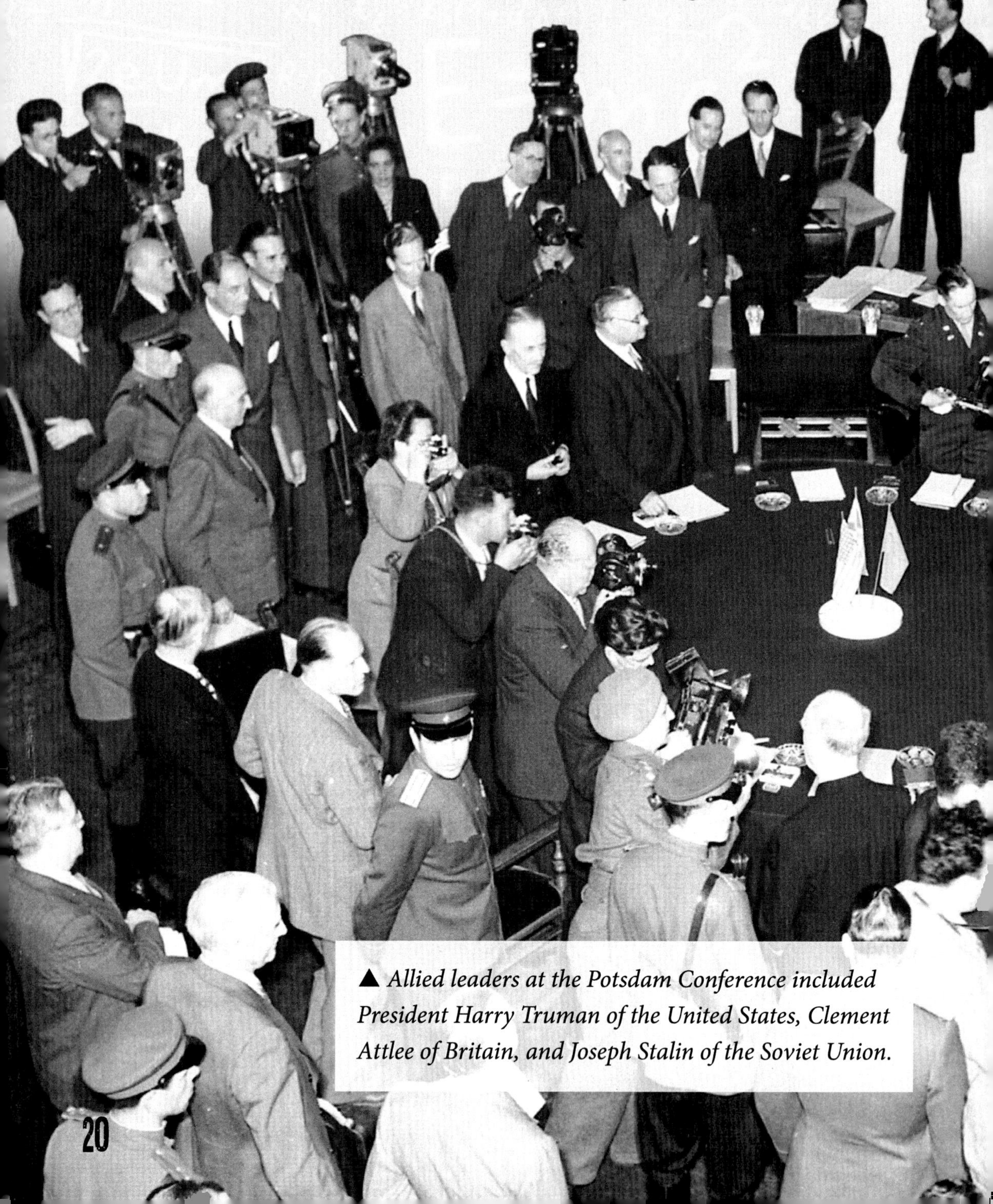

▲ *Allied leaders at the Potsdam Conference included President Harry Truman of the United States, Clement Attlee of Britain, and Joseph Stalin of the Soviet Union.*

Never Surrender!

Truman and the other leaders drew up a document known as the Potsdam Declaration. It called on Japan to **surrender** and end the war for good. If Japan refused, the Allies threatened to destroy Japan. The declaration was delivered to the Japanese on July 26, 1945. The Japanese government rejected the offer. Its army was determined to keep fighting.

"We call upon the government of Japan to proclaim now the unconditional surrender of all Japanese armed forces ... the alternative for Japan is prompt and utter destruction."

The Potsdam Declaration

surrender: to give up and admit defeat

Atomic Attack

A Difficult Decision

President Truman had a difficult decision to make. Should they use the atomic bomb? If the war continued, tens of thousands of American soldiers would probably be killed. If he dropped an atomic bomb on Japan, tens of thousands of Japanese civilians could be killed. Truman decided that to end the war as soon as possible, the atomic bomb must be used against Japan. He gave the order.

▼ *U.S. president Harry Truman was left with the terrible job of deciding whether or not to use an atomic bomb during World War II.*

Little Boy

"Little Boy" was the code name for the first-ever atomic bomb to be used during wartime. It was called this because it was thinner than other atomic bombs. Little Boy was boarded on a B-29 U.S. Air Force bomber called *Enola Gay*.

The uranium-powered atomic bomb named Little Boy had the explosive power of about 200,000 regular bombs used during World War II.

▼ *Little Boy was hardly little! It weighed 9,700 pounds (4,300 kilograms), stood over 10 feet (3 meters) tall, and had a **diameter** of 28 inches (71 centimeters).*

diameter: the distance across an object, through its center

Piloting the Plane

The *Enola Gay* was piloted by Colonel Paul Tibbets, Jr. with another 11 crew members on board. The plane took off from a U.S. air base about 1,400 miles (2,250 kilometers) away from Japan at 2 a.m. on Monday, August 6, 1945. Its target was the Japanese city of Hiroshima.

▼ *When they boarded the plane, only Tibbets (in the center here) and two other crew members knew about Little Boy. Tibbets told the others what they were carrying on their way to Hiroshima.*

Dropping the Bomb

Hiroshima was chosen because it was an industrial city. It had not been heavily bombed before and had little damage. Experts felt that they would be able to see the full effects of the A-bomb more clearly there. A timing device and change in air pressure would **activate** the bomb after it was released. Little Boy fell for 45 seconds before exploding about 1,900 feet (580 meters) above Hiroshima.

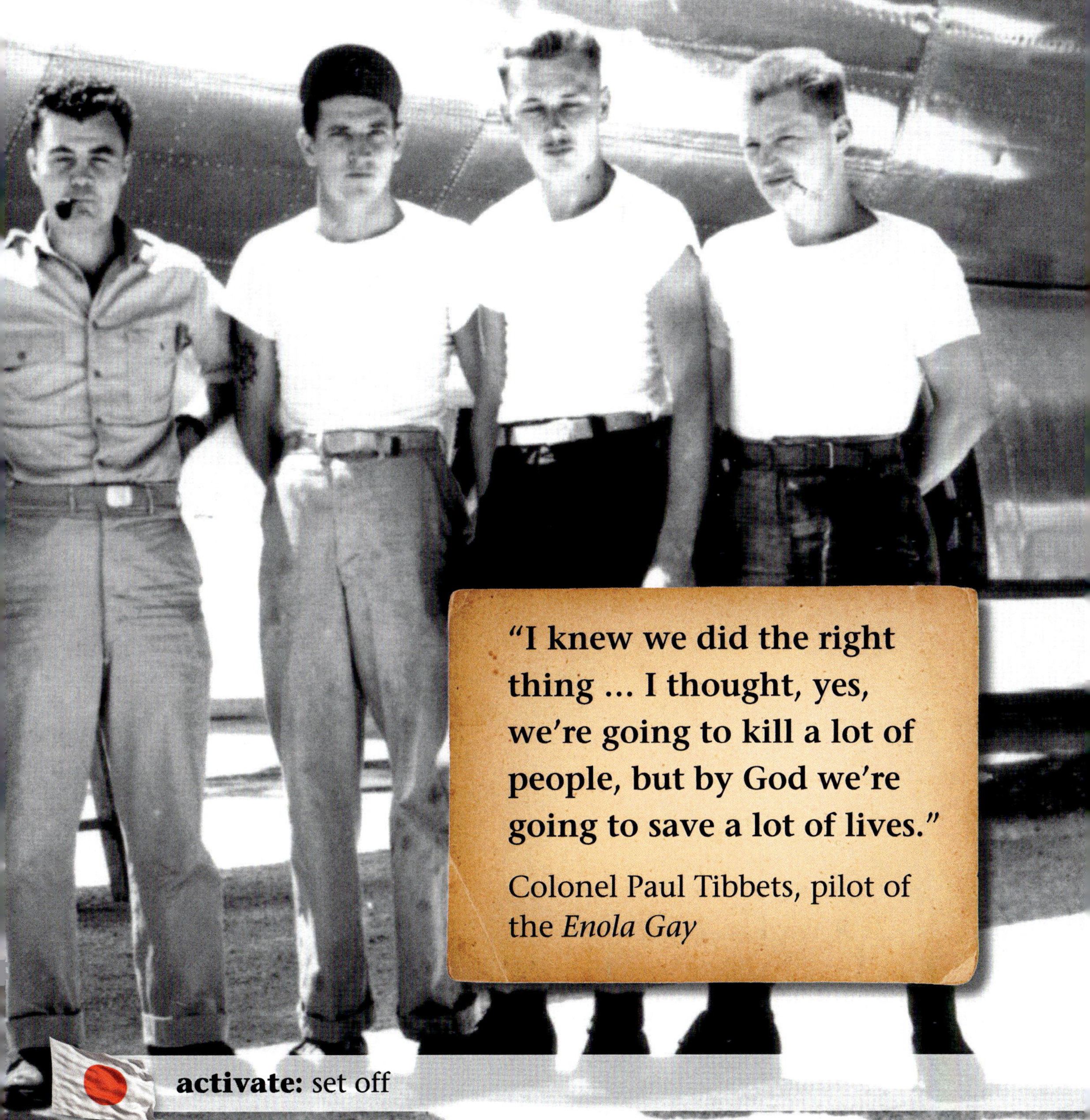

"I knew we did the right thing ... I thought, yes, we're going to kill a lot of people, but by God we're going to save a lot of lives."

Colonel Paul Tibbets, pilot of the *Enola Gay*

activate: set off

Flash Burn

The bomb exploded with a blinding flash of light. Almost immediately, a huge ball of fire began to spread over 3 miles (5 kilometers). The temperature where the bomb struck was over 5,000 °F (3,000 °C). Everything within one mile (1.6 kilometers) of the impact was vaporized instantly—humans, animals, plants, and buildings all vanished.

Destructive Winds

At the time of the atomic explosion, a powerful blast of air called a shock wave pushed outward. Strong winds traveled 7 miles (11 kilometers) in 30 seconds. Windows and doors were blown out, and even entire buildings were destroyed. Winds carrying dirt and burned waste were sucked up into a giant fireball.

▼ *Strong winds spread* ***firestorms*** *that burned trees and buildings for over 25 miles (40 kilometers) from ground zero.*

"The houses at the edge of the city ... have collapsed or burned down ... Where the city stood, there is a gigantic burned-out scar."

John Siemes, a priest

firestorm: A large, destructive fire fed by strong winds

Another A-Bomb

As the Japanese people tried to understand what had just happened in Hiroshima, the U.S. government issued a warning. If Japan did not surrender, the United States would drop another A-bomb. American aircraft dropped leaflets on cities in Japan, warning citizens of another attack. The Japanese government still refused to give in.

◀ *The B-29 Superfortress named* Bocks Car *that dropped the bomb on Nagasaki was piloted by Major Charles Sweeney.*

"My crew and I had flown to Nagasaki to end the war, not to inflict suffering."

Charles Sweeney, the pilot of the plane that dropped the bomb on Nagasaki

Fat Man and Nagasaki

Three days later, on August 9, 1945, a plutonium-powered A-bomb, code named "Fat Man," was dropped on the city of Nagasaki. Nagasaki had a thriving industry building ships for the Japanese navy. Fat Man was bigger and more powerful than Little Boy. It exploded about 1,800 feet (550 meters) above Nagasaki and its population of 260,000.

◀ *The mountains surrounding Nagasaki helped to limit the destructive effects of the atomic explosion.*

inflict: to cause something

Japan Surrenders

Even after two atomic bomb attacks, some Japanese leaders still did not want to surrender. But Japan's emperor, Hirohito, did not want his people to suffer any more. At noon on August 15, he announced to the people of Japan that their country would surrender. The war was finally over.

▼ *Despite the terrible damage at Nagasaki, many Japanese leaders felt they should continue fighting the war.*

V-J Day

On September 2, Japanese leaders signed an official document of surrender on board the U.S. Navy battleship, USS *Missouri*. The day of Japan's surrender became known as Victory over Japan Day, or V-J Day. Since the end of the war, the anniversary of V-J Day is remembered on September 2 in the United States.

▶ Japanese citizens adored their leader, Emperor Hirohito. Many believed he was a god.

"The [United States] has begun to employ a new and most cruel bomb, the power of which to do damage is, indeed, incalculable, taking the toll of many innocent lives."

Emperor Hirohito, in his speech to the Japanese people on August 15, 1945

incalculable: so great that its cost cannot be measured

Death and Destruction

Ground Zero

The atomic bomb destroyed almost all the buildings at Nagasaki within 1 mile (1.6 kilometers) of ground zero. All structures were burned or blown apart by the strength of the blast. There was even more destruction on the ground at Hiroshima. Almost all buildings within 3 miles (5 kilometers) were completely destroyed.

▼ *The low, flat ground of Hiroshima meant that the destruction of the bomb easily spread out.*

Nuclear Fallout

Even after the initial explosions, the bombs continued to cause death and destruction. Nuclear fallout is **radioactive** particles that are created during an atomic explosion. These particles get mixed in the dust and ash created by the explosion. They can be carried for miles by the strong winds. They then fall back to Earth and poison all living things.

More than 90 percent of the buildings of Hiroshima were destroyed by the atomic bomb.

radioactive: giving off harmful rays when split by fission

Instant Killer

At Hiroshima, about 45,000 people died instantly from the intense heat of the explosion. Near the site of the main blast, all living things were burned or died right away. All that was left was ash. Others died after being caught inside burning or collapsing buildings. In Nagasaki, the explosion immediately killed about 22,000 people.

▼ *This mother and child were badly burned in the bombing of Hiroshima.*

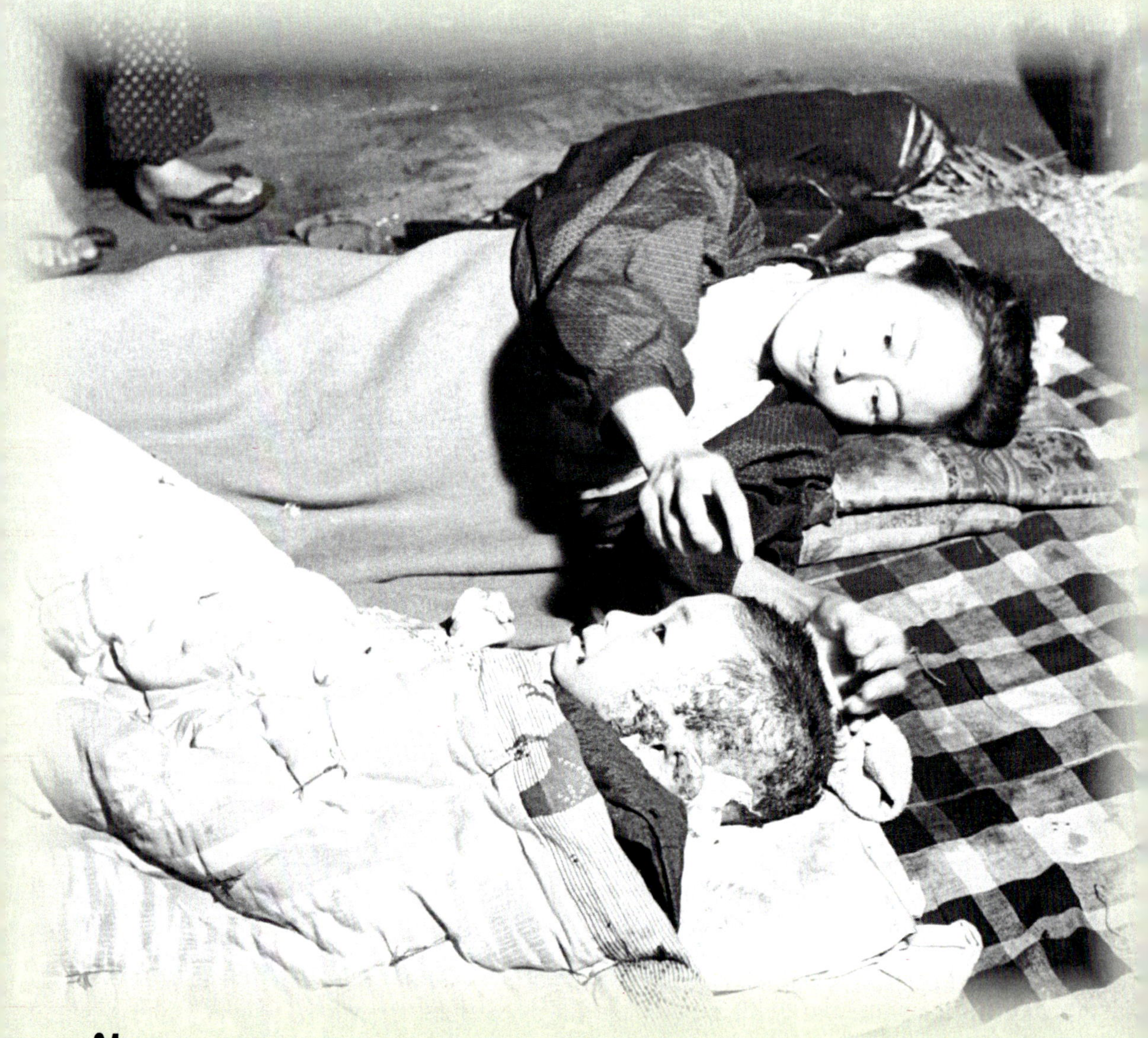

Black Rain

Radioactive particles from the bomb were pushed up into a cloud by the **afterwinds**. The cloud was carried, and cooled, by the winds. About a half an hour after the bomb exploded, a black, sticky rain fell back to Earth. The black rain spread its harmful radioactive material to even more people.

▲ *This is a child's drawing of the black rain. People did not know it would cause even more radiation poisoning.*

Radiation released from an atomic explosion is an invisible killer. It enters the cells of a person's body and can kill them days, weeks, months, or even years after the bombing.

afterwinds: strong winds caused by a bomb blast

Human Suffering

Thousands of people from Hiroshima and Nagasaki did not die instantly, but suffered from serious injuries. Some were burned by the radiation. Sometimes people's bones melted inside their bodies, causing them to become **disfigured**. Many died later from their injuries or from radiation poisoning.

▼ *Thousands of people were injured or trapped in the collapsed buildings, and there were not enough survivors to help rescue them.*

Helpless

The explosions killed many healthcare workers in both cities. They destroyed hospitals and emergency services. Thousands of people were seriously injured and needed medical attention. Many were trapped under fallen buildings—or inside burning buildings. But there were not enough people left to help those in need or to care for those who were suffering.

▶ *Hiroshima survivors still bear the scars of the atomic bomb today.*

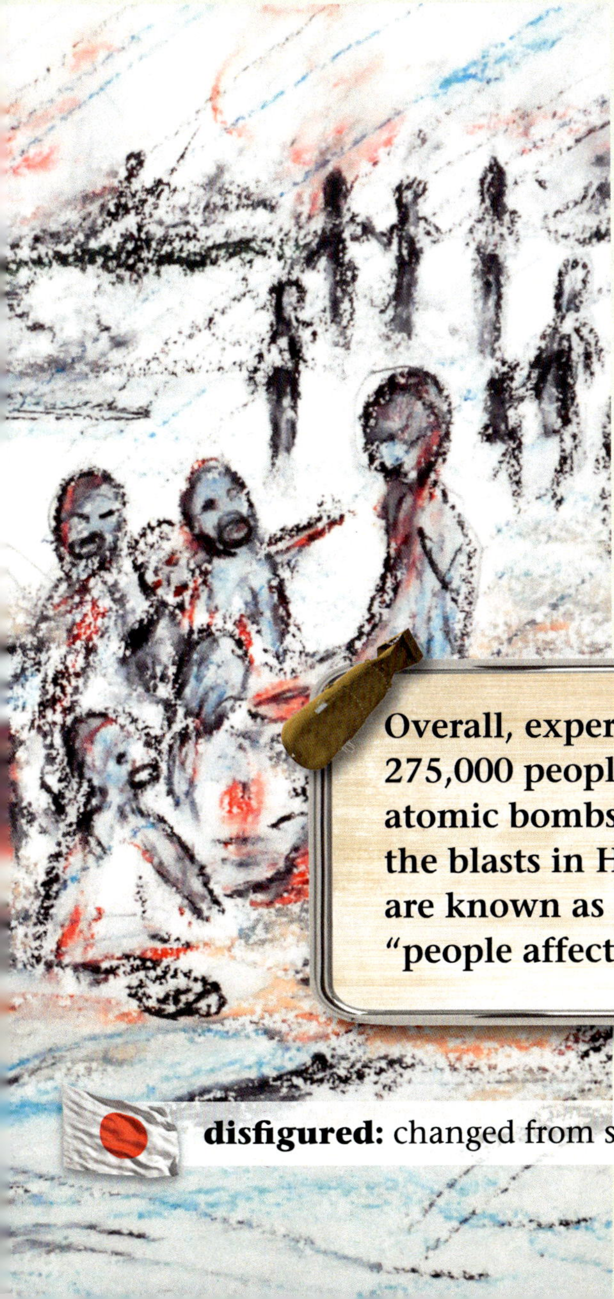

Overall, experts think that about 275,000 people died from the two atomic bombs. The people who survived the blasts in Hiroshima and Nagasaki are known as *hibakusha*, which means "people affected by the explosion."

disfigured: changed from something's usual appearance

Radiation Sickness

People from Hiroshima and Nagasaki began to fall ill from radiation sickness just a few hours after the A-bombs exploded. **Symptoms** included hair loss, bleeding in the gums and under the skin, sores and swelling in the mouth and throat, nausea, fever, weight loss, and diarrhea. Within 10 days, people started dying from the radiation poisoning.

Cancers

The horror did not end there. People developed cancers from the radiation years after the atomic bombs exploded. A young girl from Hiroshima named Sadako Sasaki was two years old when the atomic bomb was dropped. She survived the blast, but died 10 years later from a blood cancer called leukemia.

◀ *Sadako thought if she folded 1,000 paper cranes she might get better. Sadly, she died before she could finish. Today, children still put paper cranes on the peace memorial in Hiroshima.*

> **"Red spots appeared on my body, my throat hurt, I couldn't eat, I had a temperature, my gums bled, and my hair fell out. For twenty days I remained in bed, on the verge of death."**
>
> Mikiso Iwasa, a Hiroshima survivor

symptoms: signs of a particular illness or disease

Rising from the Ashes

After the Bombs

After the war ended, the United States government put together a **reconstruction** plan. American soldiers and aid workers went to Japan to help rebuild cities such as Hiroshima and Nagasaki. The new cities were even better than before. The United States also worked to make Japan's economy and government better.

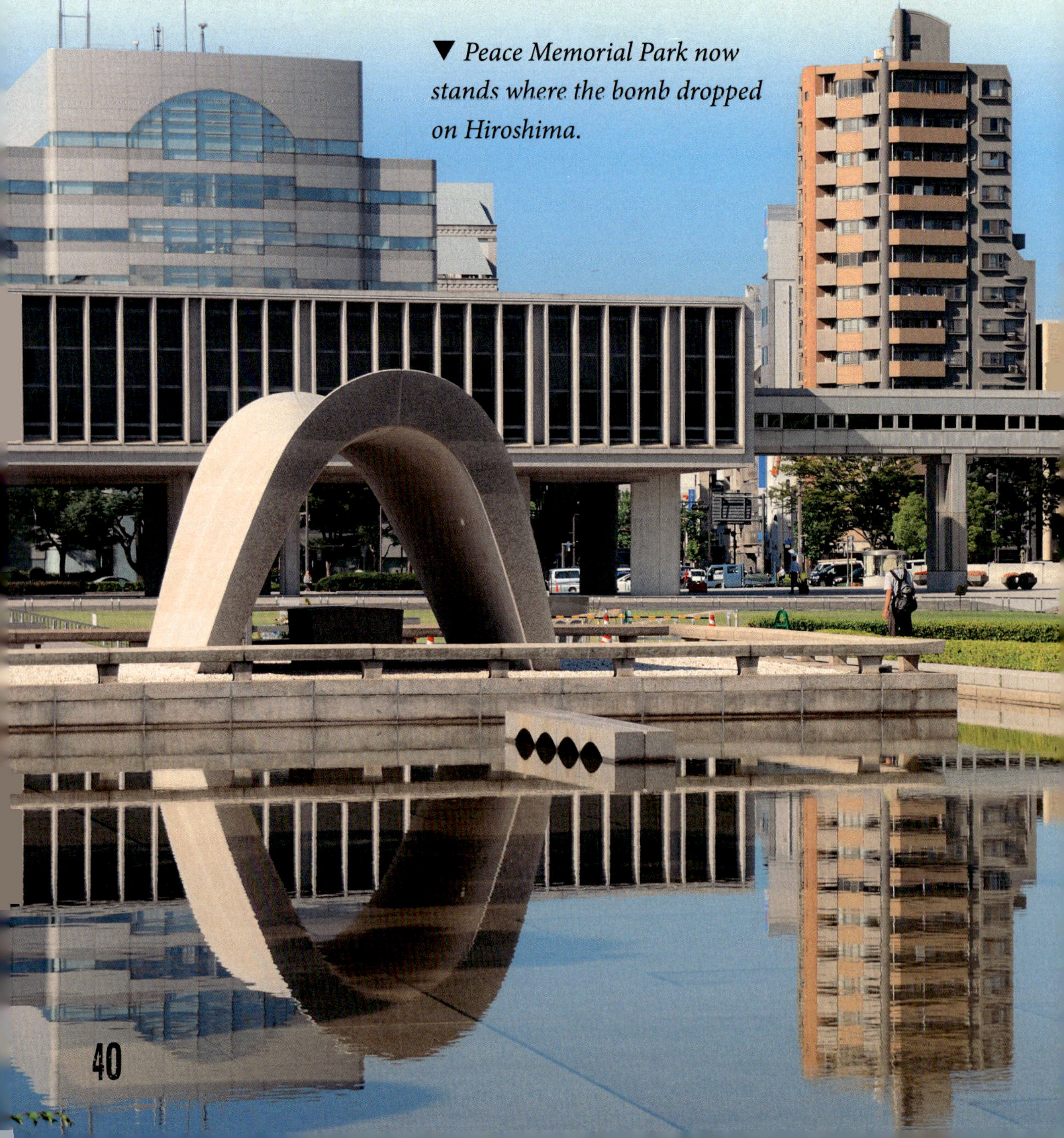

▼ *Peace Memorial Park now stands where the bomb dropped on Hiroshima.*

Peace Memorial Park

City planners wanted to rebuild Hiroshima as a city that symbolized peace. At ground zero, they built the Peace Memorial Park to honor the people who died because of the atomic bomb. The park covers about 25 acres (10 hectares) of land. It contains a museum, a Children's Peace Monument, and many other memorials.

▼ *The A-Bomb Dome was the only partially remaining building in Hiroshima after the bomb. It still stands today at Hiroshima's Peace Memorial Park.*

Every year on August 6, people gather at Peace Memorial Park. Some float colored paper lanterns in the Motoyasu River to remember those who died from the atomic bomb.

reconstruction: rebuilding

Life for the *Hibakusha*

Buildings were more easily rebuilt than the scars and injuries of the *hibakusha*. Many people faced **discrimination** after the bombings because of how they looked. A lot of them could not find work, and some were too hurt to be able to work. People did not want to marry survivors for fear their children would be born with birth defects.

▼ *This statue of a woman with her child commemorates the women victims of the bomb that fell on Nagasaki.*

The Hiroshima Maidens

In 1955, Kiyoshi Tanimoto and Norman Cousins began a project to help 25 women from Hiroshima who had been disfigured by the bomb blasts. The women were brought to New York City. Surgeons carried out 127 operations on these "Hiroshima Maidens" to improve the way they looked.

▼ *The Hiroshima Maidens were treated in the United States with plastic surgery. Hundreds of thousands of people were scarred by the bombs.*

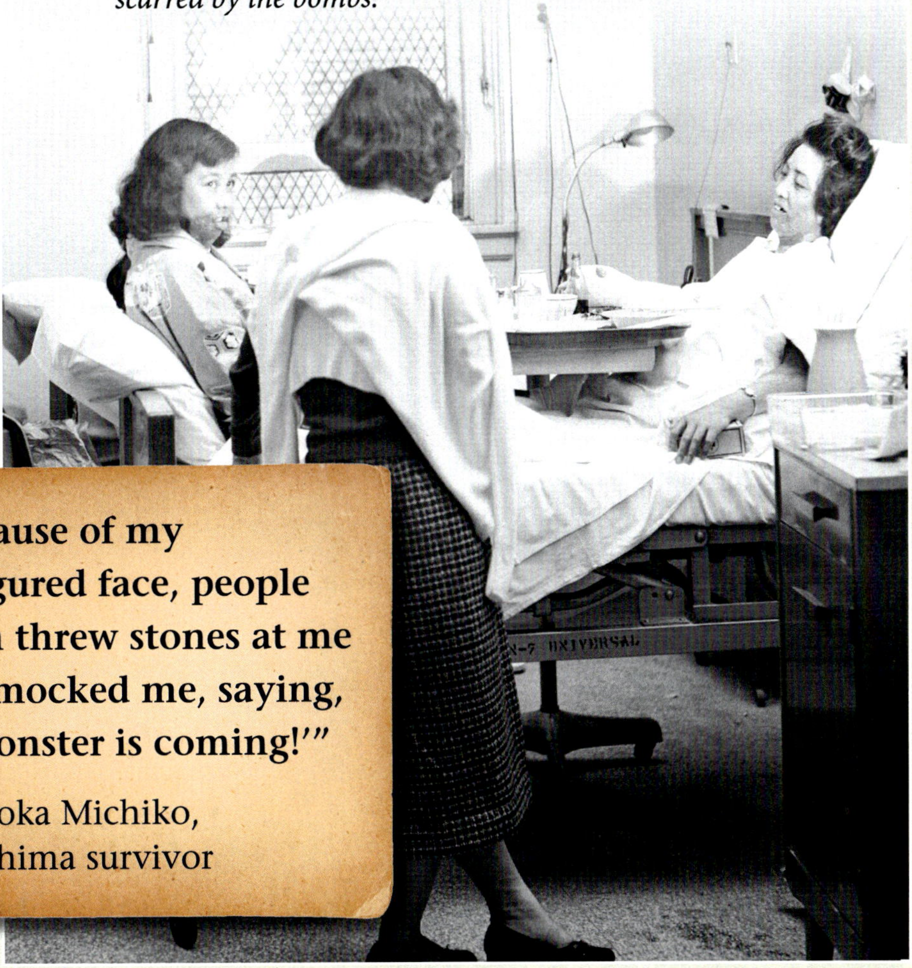

"Because of my disfigured face, people often threw stones at me and mocked me, saying, 'A monster is coming!'"

Yamaoka Michiko, Hiroshima survivor

discrimination: bad treatment

Nuclear Weapons Today

After World War II, other countries built atomic weapons, including Britain, France, and Russia. Although nuclear weapons have been tested by many nations, they have never been used again in war. It is estimated that there are about 31,000 atomic bombs in the world today. Together, they have enough power to destroy all life on Earth.

▼ *Today, atomic weapons are many times more powerful than the ones used at Hiroshima and Nagasaki.*

Modern-Day Threat

The lives of Japanese survivors were changed forever when the atomic bomb was dropped. But the bombs also changed the lives of people around the world. The fact that such powerful weapons exist in the world frightens people. Some governments and campaigners are fighting to have all nuclear weapons destroyed.

In 1996, an agreement called the Comprehensive Test Ban Treaty was adopted by the United Nations. It was an agreement to end nuclear explosions in tests or in war. Some countries, including the United States, have still not **ratified** the treaty.

ratified: formally approved and turned into a law

Learning More

Books

Hiroshima (A Place in History)
by Stewart Ross
(Arcturus Publishing, 2011)

The Manhattan Project
by Dan Elish
(Children's Press, 2007)

War in the Pacific
by Gary Jeffrey
(Crabtree Publishing, 2012)

Why Did Hiroshima Happen?
by R. G. Grant
(Gareth Stevens, 2010)

Websites

www.city.nagasaki.lg.jp/peace/english/kids/higai.html
The Nagasaki city website explains all about the effects of the bomb and how Nagasaki was rebuilt.

www.ducksters.com/history/world_war_ii/ww2_atomic_bomb.php
Information on the building and dropping of the atomic bomb

http://atomicbombmuseum.org/
The website of the Atomic Bomb Museum

Glossary

activate Set off

afterwinds Strong winds caused by a bomb blast

air-raid alarm A warning of an air attack during wartime

borough An area within a city with its own local government

diameter The distance across an object, through its center

discrimination Bad treatment

disfigured Changed from something's usual appearance

embargo A law banning trade with a particular country

evaporated Changed from a solid to a gas

firestorm A large, destructive fire fed by strong winds

incalculable So great that its cost cannot be measured

inflict To cause something

neutral Not involved in a conflict

nuclear Powered by the energy released when atoms collide

potential The power that something might have in the future

radioactive Giving off harmful rays when split by fission

ratified Formally approved and turned into a law

reconstruction Rebuilding

shortage When there is not enough of something

surrender To give up and admit defeat

symptoms Signs of a particular illness or disease

Index

Entries in **bold** refer to pictures